ISLE OF TIREE

GW01451695

CON

ABOUT

HABITA

WILDL

WALKS

ABOUT TIREE

Tiree is the outermost of the Inner Hebrides and lies around 11km west of Mull together with its sister island Coll to the north-east, which is separated from Tiree by the 4km wide Gunna Sound. The island is 19km long and roughly 5-6km wide but is remarkably flat and low-lying, except for three hills in the west, peaking at 141m on Ben Hynish. The flatness impedes drainage and there are some 37 named lochs plus numerous smaller waterbodies. There are also several streams flowing into the lochs and sea, but all are small except for An Fhaodhail, which drains southwards across the centre of the island. The island is blessed with a varied coastline. White shell sand beaches alternate between low rocky headlands, small islets and the high sea cliffs of *Ceann a' Mhara*. There is a beach that faces every wind direction with the largest stretching unbroken for 5km along the sheltered shores of Gott Bay.

Tiree's bedrock is comprised largely of ancient Lewisian Gneiss, a very hard and impervious rock, which breaks down slowly to form poor acidic soils, topped in a few places by a thin layer of peat. However, as the island is fully exposed to winds blowing off the Atlantic and is very low-lying, calcareous shell sand has been able to blow over much of the island, enriching the soils and helping to create the rich grasslands we see today.

The climate of Tiree is distinctly maritime, with the warm waters of the Gulf Stream helping to moderate the temperatures. Temperatures vary much less between summer and winter, or during the course of the day, than they do on the mainland. Frosts and snow are rare in the winter, whilst peak summer temperatures rarely exceed 20 degrees Celsius. Humidity is generally higher than on the mainland, often creating balmy evenings in the summer. Rainfall is high but not so high as on the mainland, since there are no mountains to impede the progress of rain-bearing air masses off the Atlantic. Most rain falls in winter with the driest months occurring in spring. Long cloudless days in the spring and summer months give the island its reputation for being the sunniest place in Britain. It is however, also one of Britain's windiest places, with Atlantic gales frequent in winter and strong winds possible in any month. The flat open terrain gives little relief from wind in any direction, so the island is essentially treeless, although low scrub survives where grazing pressure is less intense.

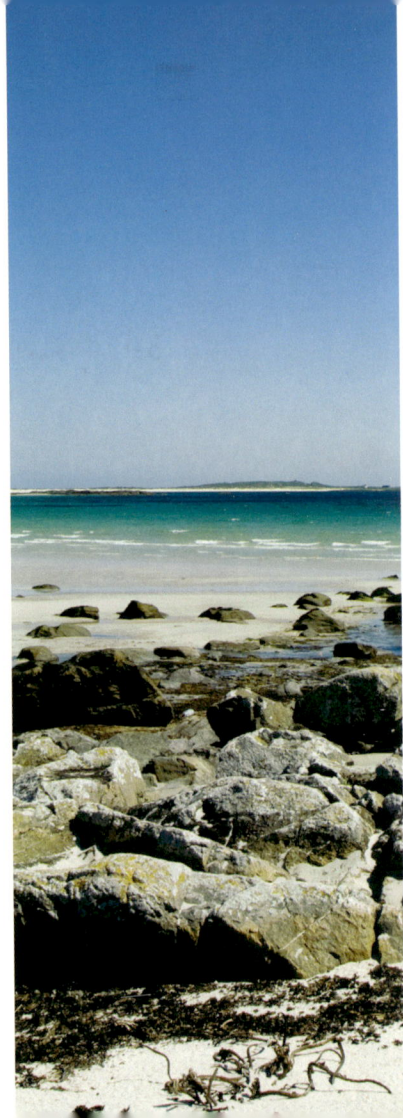

HABITATS AND PLANTS

The walks in this book have been designed to pass through a typical range of Tiree habitats and present a broad range of wildlife viewing opportunities. Coastal habitats are easily identified but those on land require closer attention as subtle changes in plant composition indicate variation in soil type, soil depth, moisture content and exposure. This is particularly true of the inland edge of the *machair*, where the influence of the lime rich shell sand varies on an intimate level with topography and lime-loving plants can be found growing close to heather and other acid-loving plants.

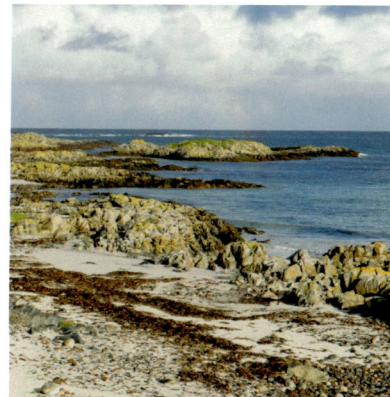

Tiree is fortunate in having bays that face in all directions so coastal birds and animals can usually find a sheltered one on all but the windiest of days. The bays are mostly shallow with sandy bottoms but all show extensive seaweed patches on submerged and coastal rocks. This wide variety of habitat proves rich feeding for marine ducks, terns, gulls and shorebirds as well as otters, seals and harbour porpoises, whilst rock pools repay closer exploration, particularly in the summer months. Typically, the western coasts are the most exposed to the elements and include the dramatic seabird breeding cliffs of *Ceann a' Mhara*, whilst there are more sheltered shores on the north-east and south-east facing coasts, which include small patches of salt marsh.

Sand blowing in off the shore has created large dune systems, particularly on the western coasts, which are stabilised by marram grass. These form the seaward edge of the *machair*, which then spreads inland highlighting the influence of windblown lime rich shell sand. In low-lying areas, such as the Reef and Vaul/Ruaig, this can spread right across the island. Tiree's *machair* is highly bio-diverse thanks to its natural fertility and generations of livestock grazing coupled with applications of seaweed. A rich variety of *machair* flowers bloom through the summer from the yellows of daisies and buttercups in April/May, to the mauves of orchids in June/July, through the reds and pinks of clover and ragged robin, to the purple of common knapweed in August/September. There are subtle variations across the *machair* in the proportions of different flowers according to topography and soil depth, whilst annual variations in rainfall and temperature mean that no two flowering summers are exactly alike. The rich profusion of *machair* flowers attract a wide range of insects, notably the rare great yellow bumblebee and northern colletes mining bee, which are largely restricted to this habitat in the UK.

In turn, the insects provide food for dense populations of breeding waders, skylarks and starlings, which are increasingly important as these species decline on the mainland.

Between the *machair* and the inland heath areas known locally as *sliabh*, lies the fenced in-bye ground. Formerly much of this land was devoted to the raising of arable crops but these days the main crop is grass silage used for feeding livestock through the winter, although some small plots of arable silage and potatoes remain, which add to habitat diversity. The in-bye grass fields range from improved rye grass swards, through damper marsh grass leys to herb rich *machair* grasslands that are cut late in the year. Sensitive management of these fields by Tiree's crofters and farmers involving late and friendly cutting has allowed the rare corncrake to thrive here. After the cutting in late summer, the short grass fields provide rich feeding for waders, gulls and starlings, whilst large numbers of waders breed on them in the spring.

Inland areas away from the influence of the shell sand have a wetter more acidic soil and are often rocky with patches of heather and extensive bogs and small lochans. This is the Tiree *sliabh*, which harbours a range of interesting plants such as the sundews and butterworts that capture insects to gain additional nutrients. Traditional practices of low intensity grazing, rush cutting and liming have enriched areas to the benefit of wildlife. Rocky knolls are home to a fascinating diversity of plants including ferns and even stunted willows in some places, whilst patches of gorse planted to act as fences and windbreaks provide nesting areas for stonechats and linnets. The bogs are home to high densities of breeding snipe and smaller numbers of dunlin, as well as inland gull colonies, nesting here in the absence of ground predators such as foxes and mink. Small pools here also harbour the full range of Tiree's damselflies and dragonflies. Tiree has no real native woodland but isolated patches of planted bushes and stunted trees in gardens and elsewhere, act as magnets for tired migrants and for breeding garden birds.

Corncrake

Snipe

WILDLIFE THROUGH THE YEAR ON TIRE

The walks are worthy of exploration at all times of year, since the wildlife seen will vary considerably with the seasons. A few species such as rock pipits and oystercatchers on the rocky shore, lapwings and starlings on the grasslands and snipe in the wetlands are present all year-round, but most species are highly seasonal.

The winter months generally bring the harshest weather, with frequent gales and rain, so good walking days are at a premium. However, wildlife watching at this time of year can be spectacular and you will frequently have the paths to yourself. Huge flocks of barnacle geese frequent the Ringing Stone and Ruaig areas with smaller groups elsewhere, whilst elusive Greenland white-fronts feed in rushy areas on the edge of the *sliabh*. Large herds of whooper swans frequent the lochs, particularly Loch a' Phuill, where they are joined by throngs of wigeon, teal, tufted duck and goldeneye. Nationally important numbers of ringed plovers, sanderling, turnstones and purple sandpipers feed along the shore and do not be surprised to see large flocks of turnstones feeding well inland on the grasslands with golden plovers, lapwing and curlew. Winter gales from the northwest in the New Year bring small numbers of glaucous and Iceland gulls to the beaches, particularly if there are dead seals about. Calmer bays are worth searching for wintering great northern and red-throated divers, whilst amongst the widespread eiders and red-breasted mergansers look out for long-tailed ducks and common scoters. Rare sea-beans may also wash ashore, having travelled from the Caribbean on the Gulf Stream and more rarely are joined by young sea turtles that have drifted too far north.

Small numbers of meadow pipits, pied wagtails and twite winter on the island, but as days lengthen in February many more return to breed here and are joined in March by the first linnets and passage white wagtails. Large numbers of black-headed and lesser black-backed gulls return in March and often bring the odd rarer gull with them, whilst whooper swans stream overhead on their way back to Iceland. April sees the return of many breeding migrant birds including the first corncrakes, terns, wheatears and willow warblers, whilst the wintering Greenland geese head north for their Arctic breeding grounds midmonth.

Pied wagtail

Redshank

In warm springs, the first lapwing broods emerge in April and snipe start drumming once more in the wetlands. Huge numbers of golden plover build up on the island during the month, before setting off north, and are joined around the loch edges by passage flocks of whimbrel and black-tailed godwits – the latter in their resplendent brick red breeding dress. Big flocks of pale-bellied brent geese also stop off to refuel on green seaweed in the bays before heading on up to Iceland and then on again to breed in Greenland. April also sees brown hares boxing in the fields and the first butterflies emerge on warmer days, whilst as the seas slowly warm up, the first harbour porpoises appear around the coast.

May marks the start of the main breeding period for ground nesting birds, so please be careful not to disturb nests and always move away from alarm calling parent birds, since their eggs or chicks will be nearby. This is the best month to see corncrakes as the vegetation is still short and the calling males often fight over the best territories. Equally, most breeding migrant birds will be back in and singing, including a handful of cuckoos, whilst high Arctic nesting waders such as dunlin, ringed plover and sanderling move through on the beaches in their thousands. Easterly winds in May can bring scarcer migrants that do not breed here such as spotted flycatcher and redstart, as well as occasional rarities. The first dragonflies emerge this month and join an increasing variety of butterflies on the wing, whilst the first dolphins, minke whales and basking sharks appear offshore. Although the first flowers appear in April, May sees a greater variety appearing and many will be different to those that appear later in the summer.

Bird migration tails off in June, as the local breeding birds tend to their first broods, including a mass synchronised hatch of young starlings at the very start of the month. Corncrake calling reaches its zenith this month and it is well worth walking down one of the small roads in West Tiree around midnight on a calm mild night to hear them at their best. This is also a great month to walk up onto the headland of *Ceann a' Mhara* to see, hear and smell the seabird breeding season there in full flow. The *machair* starts blooming more profusely in June and the *sliabh* pools are alive with dragonflies and specialist flowering plants. Common seals have their pups this month and are easily seen on skerries at West Hynish and Salum, whilst there are increasing numbers of dolphins and basking sharks offshore.

Black-tailed godwits

July and August see the *machair* blooming at its finest and it attracts peak numbers of bumblebees, mining bees, moths and butterflies at this time. Fortunately, Tiree is generally too windy for midges to be much of a nuisance, although horseflies can be problematic on the warmest days. High summer normally sees greatest numbers of basking sharks offshore and, with luck, they may be joined by killer whales. Look out for large gatherings of feeding terns, Manx shearwaters, auks and gannets offshore as these often form over feeding cetaceans. Many smaller breeding birds will be on their second broods by now but the young seabirds will mostly fledge this month. Flocks of locally reared lapwings, oystercatchers, gulls and starlings find rich pickings on the first of the cut grass silage fields and are joined by the first passage golden plovers, black-tailed godwits and ruff. Flocks of post breeding dunlin, ringed plover and sanderling reappear on the beaches and greenshank grace the loch edges, whilst flocks of local breeding twite and linnets feast on the seedheads of uncut meadows and *machair*.

September is the peak month for passage birds on the island. Swallow flocks build up on the wires prior to departure, large numbers of meadow pipits and wheatears pass through from further north and scarcer migrants such as pied flycatcher and lesser whitethroat can turn up in isolated bush patches. Onshore gales this month can bring huge numbers of seabirds streaming past headlands at Hynish and Balevullin. Local auks, fulmars and kittiwakes are joined by throngs of Manx shearwaters, together with smaller numbers of sooty shearwaters, storm petrels, grey phalaropes, skuas and the occasional Sabine's gull. Strong westerlies can also bring vagrant waders from North America, small numbers of which appear annually this month amongst the swelling golden plover flocks on the *machair* and along the loch shores. September sees the last of the *machair* blooms and numbers of bumblebees and butterflies drop away.

October sees the return of our avian winter visitors. Barnacle geese and Greenland white-fronts return once more and huge numbers of whooper swans stop over to feed on the lochs, although most will head on to spend the winter further south. Northeast winds bring large flocks of redwings and fieldfares, as well as smaller numbers of siskins, goldfinches, redpolls and bramblings. Passing blackcaps, goldcrests and chiffchaffs feed up in the bushy gardens and are often joined by the odd rarity from further east such as a yellow-browed warbler or red-breasted flycatcher.

Great yellow bumblebee

Six-spot burnet moth

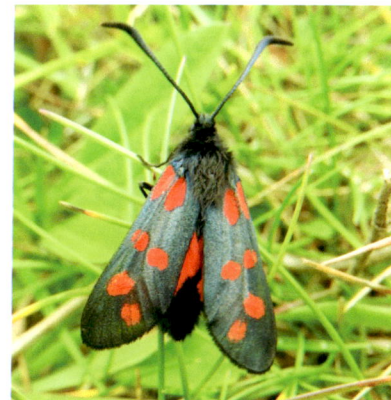

In late October, gales from the west often bring the odd rare duck across from North America such as an American wigeon, green-winged teal or ring-necked duck, which join the growing numbers of teal, wigeon and tufted ducks on the lochs. Despite the increasingly stormy weather, this is the month that the grey seals have their pups on the offshore skerries.

November and December see regular gales and the winter birds hunker down for their short, wet and windy, but usually frost-free, days. Winter storms cast huge banks of seaweed onto the shores, which provide rich feeding grounds for the wintering shorebirds, starlings and gulls. Certain sheltered beaches see heaps of multi-coloured seashells washed ashore, mostly limpets and mussels, but including delicate yellow and maroon coloured periwinkles, and porcelainlike cowries. Small numbers of snow buntings feed around the shores in some winters, often in the company of wintering twite. Flooding of low lying grasslands creates good feeding opportunities for lapwings, golden plovers and dabbling duck, whilst sheltered gardens provide winter homes for robins, dunnocks and chaffinches, none of which breed on Tiree. All of these wintering birds must run the gauntlet of high densities of wintering raptors including merlins, sparrowhawks, kestrels, peregrines, hen harriers and buzzards, whilst short-eared and barn owls appear in some years.

In short, Tiree warrants exploration at all times of year in order to gain a full appreciation of its habitats and wildlife, as well as its dynamic weather. All of the walks are of interest year-round but the timing of key wildlife is also detailed in the path descriptions. You are unlikely to see everything on a single trip even in the correct season, so repeated visits are recommended.

12

High Water Mark

Low Water Mark

Sand

START HERE

Am Barradhu

Hynish Centre

HYNISH

Hynish House

Millport House

Gasamull

Clèit Mhòr

Happy Valley

Bogha Mòr

An Snoig

N

Happy Valley from Hynish Centre
Haoidhnis gu Lag na Clèit

A short, easy walk on relatively flat ground from the Hynish Centre along the coast to the beautiful and peaceful Happy Valley.

Leave your car in the area to the left of the gate at the Hynish Centre. There are public toilets at the Skerryvore Lighthouse exhibition.

Please keep dogs under control, preferably on a leash.

The Hynish centre houses two exhibitions: the Skerryvore Lighthouse which details the building of the tallest lighthouse in Scotland and the Treshnish Isles which describes the geology, history and natural history of the islands visible from the east coast of Tiree.

Follow the road uphill for a short distance past Hynish House. A track then takes you on through a couple of fields towards Millport House. Passing through a gate, the track then turns towards the coast in front of Millport House and over a stile. Walk towards the coast and turn right over a small stream.

The path turns into a farm track that crosses a series of pebbled areas. Follow the farm track until it arrives at a series of rocky outcrops. Turn right uphill for a short distance and you will arrive at the mouth of the valley. An easy walk on an obvious path takes you down towards the sea.

It is not clear how Happy Valley got its name. It is widely held that the name derives from WWII when the island airport was used for reconnaissance flights and over 2,000 airmen were stationed on Tiree.

Walk Details

Total Distance	1.9 miles / 3 km
Total Duration	1 hour

Terrain Description
Short, moderate slopes. Mostly smooth grassy paths with some uneven sections which can be muddy after heavy rain.

A

Location

Happy Valley

easy

Wildlife Watch

This walk passes through a variety of different habitats including in-bye grassland, *machair*, wet grassland and rocky coast – it offers the chance of seeing a wide range of wildlife. Listen out for the rasping call of corncrakes in the in-bye grassland from May to July.

Grey and common seals frequent the rocky offshore skerries, whilst the tall fins of basking sharks can be spotted, from time to time on calm summer days, cruising the inshore waters. Otters are also present here but patience and luck are required for a sighting.

A colony of Arctic terns nests on the beach below Millport House from May to July. They are very susceptible to disturbance and the adults will defend their nests and dive-bomb you if you get too close. Please view them from a safe distance and walk away from the area if they start to fly towards you.

A few pairs of sand martins nest in burrows in the sandy cliffs along the small stream, whilst the wet grassland beyond holds many breeding waders in late spring including noisy redshanks and oystercatchers, which will scold you if they have a nest nearby. A colony of common gulls nest in the marsh behind Millport House, whilst fulmars nest on the higher cliffs and crags.

Wheatears favour the short turf of Happy Valley, nesting in the rocky crags above, whereas rock pipits haunt the seaweed strewn shore. Keep an eye out for both shags and great northern divers feeding in the waters off the beach at Happy Valley.

A wide range of smaller creatures can also be seen on calm sunny summer days. Butterflies to watch out for along the route include common blue, small tortoiseshell, red admiral, green-veined white and meadow brown, whilst painted ladies can be abundant here during invasion years. Delicate blue-tailed damselflies frequent the streams and highland darter dragonflies perch on sheltered sun facing rocks. Bumblebees thrive on the herb rich grasslands and include the bright orange and yellow coloured moss carder bee. In addition, two species of mining bee make their breeding burrows in the sandy soil on the coastal fringe.

Features of this Walk

During the walk, look out for seals on and around the offshore rocks. Otters have also been seen here but are elusive. On the hill above the beach are the remains of an ancient hill fort. Look out for the natural arches and blowholes on the west side of the bay. Arctic terns nest on the beach just below Millport House - please give them a wide berth to avoid disturbing them.

Wheatear

Moss carder bee

Arctic tern

Redshank

Sometimes known as 'the warden of the marshes'.
Redshanks are alert noisy birds that will scold you if
you approach them too closely. Breeding birds will
often perch on roadside fence posts as they keep
watch over their family. They remain widespread in
the wetlands and loch sides of Tiree, but have
declined on the mainland in recent years. Larger
flocks stop off in spring and autumn en route to and
from breeding grounds in Iceland.

Corncrake

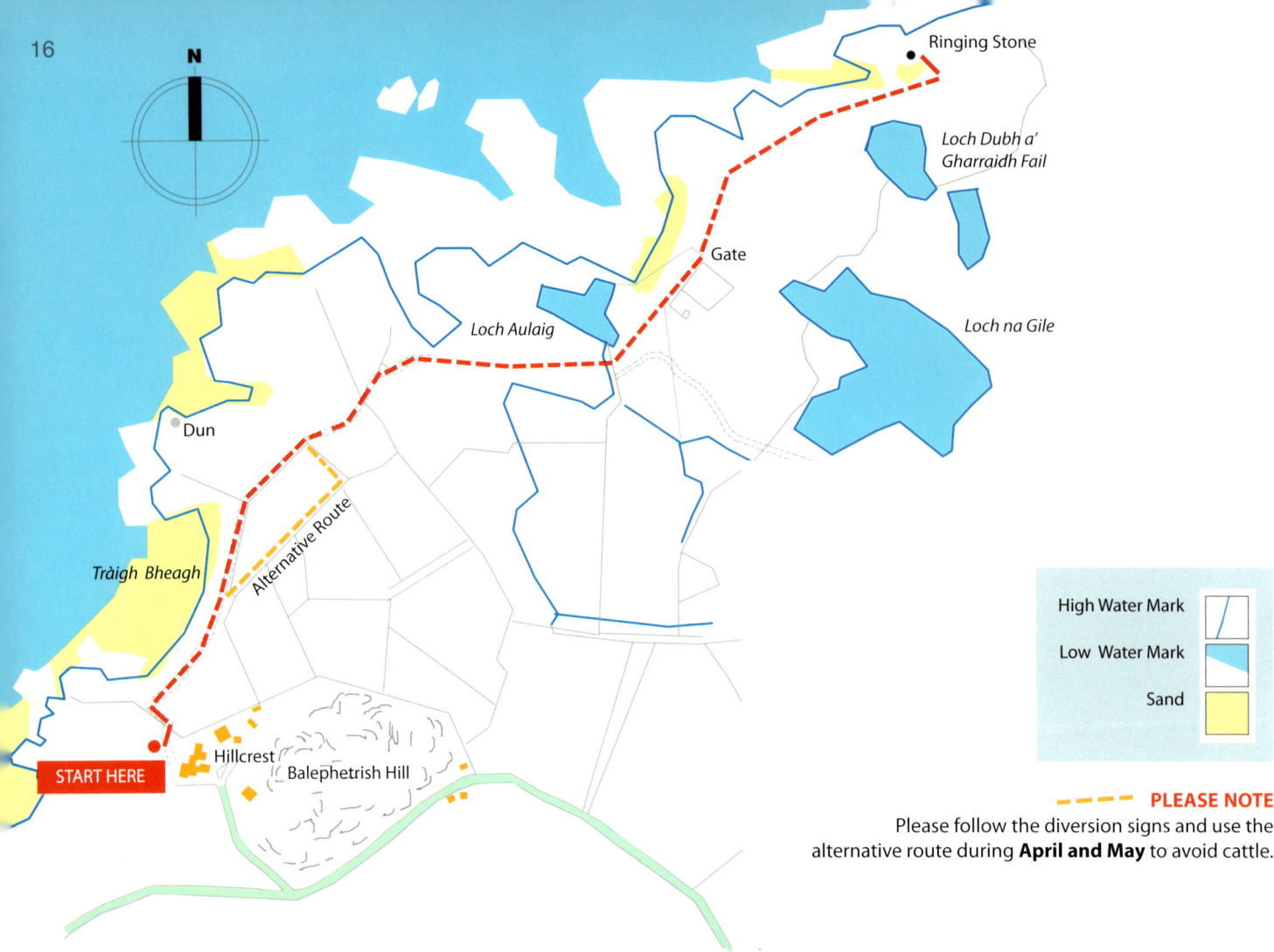

N

Ringing Stone

Loch Dubh a'
Gharraidh Fail

Gate

Loch na Gile

Loch Aulaig

Dun

Tràigh Bheagh

Alternative Route

START HERE

Hillcrest

Balephetrish Hill

	High Water Mark	
Low Water Mark	
Sand	

PLEASE NOTE

Please follow the diversion signs and use the
alternative route during **April and May** to avoid cattle.

Ringing Stone from Hillcrest
Taigh Bhaile Phèadrais gu Clach a' Choire

B

A moderate length walk on relatively flat ground from Hillcrest along the coast to the Ringing Stone.

Leave your car at the parking area to the left of the gate behind Hillcrest House.

Go through the gate, turn sharp left. Follow the track towards the bay then turn right and follow the track past a ruin. At the end of the bay turn right through a gate with a white arrow on the left hand gatepost. Go up a gentle incline with a fence on the right. At the end of the fence the track veers right then back left to a gate with a white arrow on the right hand gatepost.

Go through the gate and walk straight on, and then bear right following the track along a grassy promontory. Cross a small bridge over a stream, just before the next gate with a white arrow on the left hand gatepost. Go through the gate and follow a meandering track to another gate with a green circle with a white arrow and 360m on the left hand gatepost. Beyond the gate you enter open grassland and the track narrows.

Follow this single track, crossing a stream with a firm pebbly bottom. This stream can become wide after heavy rain. Where the single track splits into two, take the right hand track and follow this until you meet a raised rocky promontory with Loch Dubh a' Gharraidh Fail on your right. There can be a stream or water here to bypass after heavy rain. Continue straight on over the rocky promontory and you will see the Ringing Stone on the left, near the shore. Don't be tempted to take a shortcut directly to the Stone as there is a sea inlet on the left of the rocky promontory.

Ringing Stone

Walk Details

Total Distance	2.7 miles / 4.3 km
Total Duration	2 hours

Terrain Description
Relatively flat ground with short, moderate slopes. Mostly smooth, grassy paths with some uneven sections. Can be muddy after heavy rain.

easy

Wildlife Watch

This walk passes through a variety of different habitats including *machair*, in-bye grassland, moorland (known locally as *sliabh*), wet grassland, sandy bays and rocky coast – it offers the chance of seeing a wide range of wildlife.

From the parking area, look for the fulmars that nest on the cliff face of the old quarry at Balephetrish Hill, where they are sometimes joined by a pair of ravens. Grey and common seals frequent the bays and haul out on the rocky offshore skerries, whilst on calm summer days, small groups of harbour porpoises feed just offshore and if you are lucky you may spot the tall fins of basking sharks seeking out their plankton diet in the inshore waters. Otter footprints can often be seen on the sandy shore of Traigh Bheagh but seeing the animals themselves requires luck. This beach often holds a range of shorebirds, depending on the month, including sanderling and dunlin in May whilst oystercatchers and ringed plovers are present year round. Listen out for the rasping call of corncrakes in the in-bye grassland and iris beds from May to July, and the twittering song of skylarks.

Small colonies of Arctic terns nest on rocky headlands close to the shore from May to July, whilst the nests of waders and gulls are dotted along this route. Please try to stick to the path during the breeding season to avoid disturbing the birds and view them from a safe distance. The parent birds will scold you if they have a nest nearby and you are too close. The lochs along the route normally hold a few ducks including eider, shelduck and mallard as well as greylag geese. In winter these coastal grasslands are home to a large flock of barnacle geese. Wheatears favour the short coastal turf near the Ringing Stone and rock pipits can normally be found along the rocky shore. Gannets can often be seen feeding offshore here and in late spring it is worth searching amongst the feeding shags for late great northern divers in resplendent breeding dress.

Calm sunny summer days are the best for looking for insects. Butterflies to watch out for here include the common blue, green-veined white and meadow brown. Four-spotted chaser dragonflies hold territory over the moorland pools, whilst common blue damselflies frequent the streams. Look out for bumblebees wherever there are flowers. The *machair* west of Hillcrest is one of the best on the island for bees, including the rare great yellow bumblebee, which even here is outnumbered by the black and red coloured red-shanked carder bee and the orange and yellow moss carder bee.

Features of this Walk

During the walk, look out for seals in the bays and on and around the offshore rocks. Otter sightings are also possible here but they are elusive – look for their tracks on the sandy beach of Traigh Bheagh. On the rocky ground to the seaward side of the track are the remains of an ancient fort or "dun". Look out for the natural arches just west of the start of the walk. Arctic terns nest on rocky headlands beyond Traigh Bheagh and Loch Aulaig - please give them a wide berth to avoid disturbing them during the breeding season.

Meadow brown

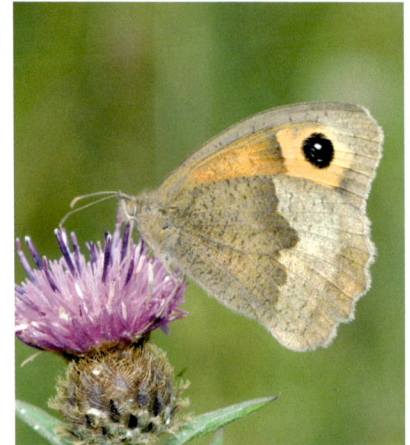

Gannet

Our largest seabird, adults are boldly white with black wingtips and a yellow tinged head, whilst young birds are mottled darker. All show distinctive long pointed wings and a pale daggerlike bill. They glide low over the water, often travelling in small groups but feed on fish by flying up high and plunging at speed into the sea. Watch out for the splashes of diving birds on calmer days. The nearest major breeding colonies to Tiree are on Ailsa Craig to the south and St Kilda to the north, although a small colony has recently established nearby on Barra Head.

Dunlin

Arctic terns

Barnacle goose

Ringed plover

N

Sgeir Bharrach

Loch an Fhaing

Dun Mor Broch

Dun Beag Fo

START HERE

Stile

Am Beannan Ruadh

Stile

Rhum View

Stile

Creag na Cradh-gheòidh

Ringing Stone

VAUL

Loch Dubh

Loch Dubh a' Gharraidh Fail

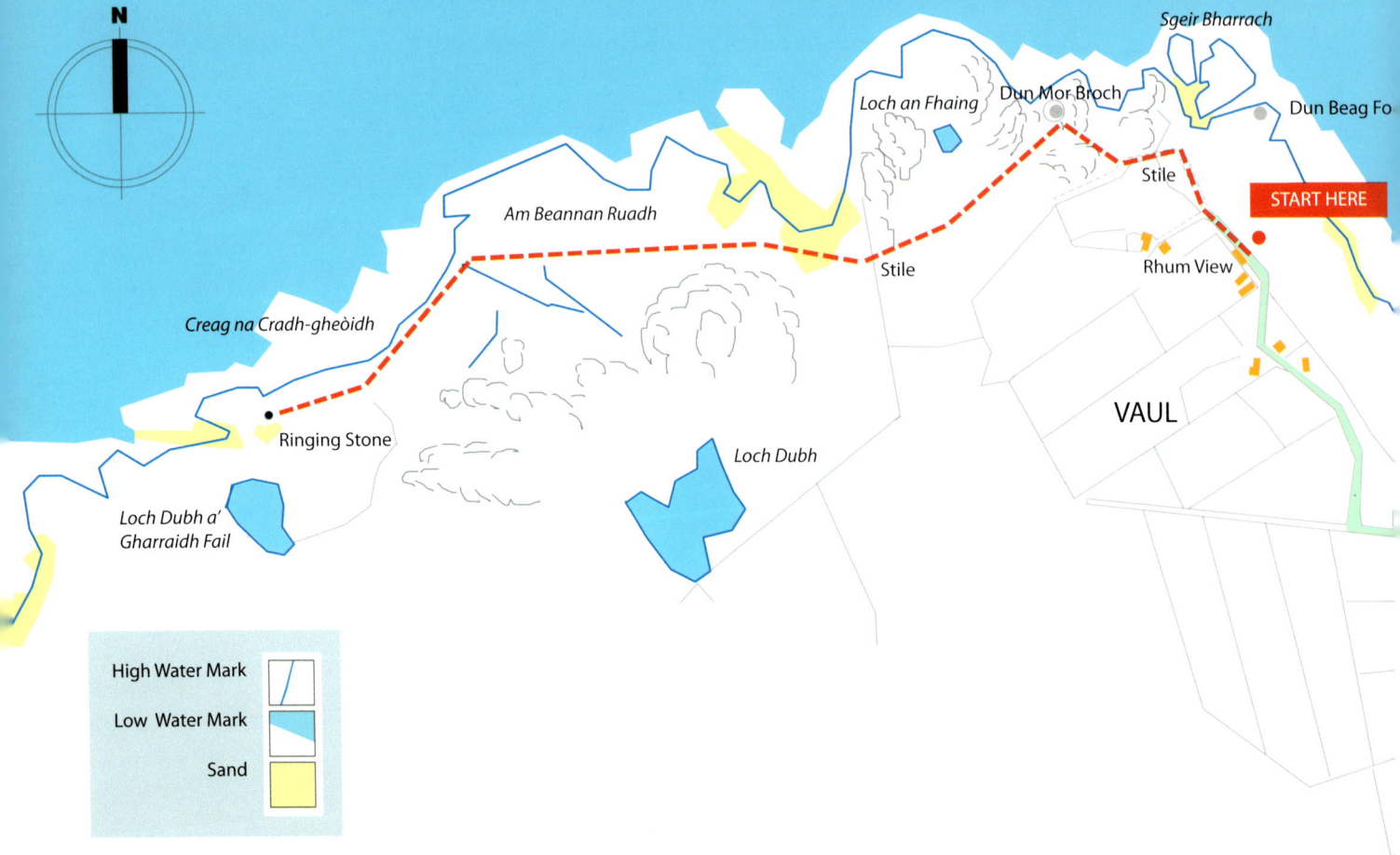

High Water Mark	
Low Water Mark	
Sand	

Ringing Stone from Upper Vaul
Bràigh Bhalla gu Clach a' Choire

C

A medium length walk on sometimes uneven and marshy ground from Upper Vaul along the coast to the Ringing Stone.

Leave your car in the small grassed area to the right of the road opposite the house called Rhum View. There is a trig point on the right just before the parking area.

Follow the track from the car park downhill towards the sea. At the bottom of the hill turn left and cross a stile by a gate. There is an information board for Dun Mor Broch here. To visit the Broch follow posts to the right. The post on the top of the rocky mound in the distance marks the Broch.

To continue to the Ringing Stone follow the track uphill after the stile. At the top of the hill veer right - you'll see a large stone cairn on your right. Aim towards the rocky sections before the sea and just before reaching these turn left. Continue straight on, aiming for a dry stone wall with a fence on top. As you approach this you will find a drainage ditch. Keep the ditch on your right and then cross a stream. Once over the stream you will see a stile in the wall with a marker post with green arrow. Cross the stile and follow the direction of the green arrow passing a small beach. At the end of the beach turn right. After about 20m turn left and follow the track slightly uphill past the 'lazy beds' on your left. Beyond the 'lazy beds' the track becomes rougher. When the track forks, keep left and then straight on, keeping rocky outcrops to your right.

Eventually the track veers right toward the sea and meets a stream. Cross the stream then follow the track past a small sandy inlet. Continue straight on, passing what appear to be the remains of an old square water tank. The track skirts a grass promontory. Continue on until you see a notice board in the distance off to the right. The Ringing Stone is opposite this towards the sea.

Walk Details

Total Distance	2.8 miles / 4.5 km
Total Duration	2 hours

Terrain Description
Relatively flat ground with short, moderate slopes. Mostly smooth, grassy paths with some uneven sections. Can be muddy after heavy rain.

Location

Dun Mor Broch

moderate

Wildlife Watch

Scan the sea from the parking area and the Broch, there are sometimes basking sharks and harbour porpoises present offshore in summer, together with common seals on the offshore rocks. Killer Whales have very occasionally been seen here looking for unwary seals! The rocky heathery area around the Broch often holds a few twite in summer and the white rumps of wheatears are sure to be seen as the birds fly ahead of you. The small, sandy bay ahead usually has the odd pair of attendant oystercatchers, whilst the nearby *machair* holds frog orchids in late summer, contrasting with the bog loving heath spotted-orchids and bog asphodels on the adjacent moorland. The furrows here in the moor are the remains of so-called 'lazy beds' which would have been thoroughly hard work from which to raise a crop of corn or potatoes.

The marshy pools on the left, after you round the rocky crag of Creagan Mora, are the remains of old peat cuttings. A few pairs of eiders nest here, whilst the cuttings themselves are good for dragonflies such as the four-spotted chaser and the highland darter. Pied wagtails and rock pipits can normally be found along the rocky shore and in the spring are joined by migrating white wagtails on their way north to Iceland. Gannets can often be seen feeding offshore from the Ringing Stone and in late spring it is worth searching amongst the feeding shags for late great northern divers in their resplendent breeding dress.

Calm sunny summer days are the best for looking for insects. Butterflies to watch out for on the route include the common blue, green-veined white and meadow brown, plus small tortoiseshell and red admiral around sheltered nettle clumps at the start of the walk. The old peat cuttings and moorland pools are home to all three of Tiree's resident dragonflies. Four-spotted chasers emerge first in late May followed by highland and black darters later in the summer, with all three species present on sunny days in July. The rock pools behind the Ringing Stone are full of seashore life in summer. The deeper ones hold shore crabs, prawns and blennies, as well as sea anemones and a range of sea snails.

Features of this Walk

During the walk, keep an eye out for seals in the bays and on and around the offshore rocks. Otters have also been seen here but they are elusive. Dun Mor Broch is the most complete ancient fortified dwelling house on Tiree and is well worth visiting. Look out for the second and more ruined Dun Beag Fort to the SE of the broch.

Heath spotted-orchid

Four-spotted chaser

Frog orchid

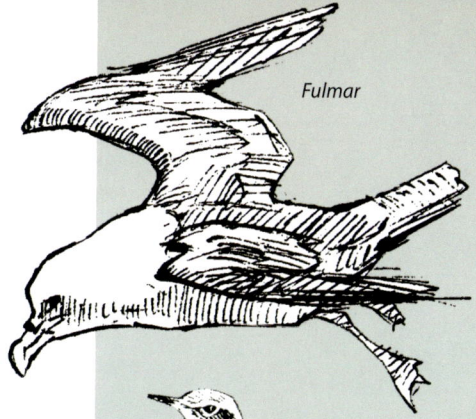

Fulmar

Wheatear

Pied wagtail

Unlike on the mainland, pied wagtails are summer visitors to Tiree with only one or two birds spending the winter around the coast. Large numbers return in March and they breed all over the island, with family parties a common roadside sight in high summer. The black and white plumage and long wagging tail is distinctive, although the very similar, but greyer, white wagtail also occurs in large numbers in April and May on its way to Iceland.

Eider

START HERE

Tràigh Mhòr

Loch Riaghain

High Water Mark

Low Water Mark

Sand

N

Loch Dubh a' Gharraidh Fail

Loch nan Ob

Loch na Gile

Cru Lochanan

Ringing Stone from Gott Bay
Loch Ghot gu Clach a' Choire

D

A medium length walk on relatively flat but sometimes marshy and flooded ground from Gott Bay to the Ringing Stone.

Location

Gott Bay

After turning onto the road signposted Gott, park immediately on the right.

Follow the road past a cattle grid and then through a gate. Turn right and veer left past a small felt-roofed house. Walk straight ahead towards the loch, keeping the large, white house on your right. Follow the path along the loch shore to an old gate.

Beyond the gate the track turns right. After heavy rain this section of the track can be flooded. Continue on the track, passing under telegraph poles. The path veers left as it meets a fence and goes on to a gate.

Continue on the path between two lochans. Veer left at Loch na Gile after which a stream crosses the track. The stream can flood after heavy rain. Cross the stream and continue along the track until a fence is reached. Turn right and follow the fence until a gate is found. On the gate post is a green circle with white arrow and the writing '360m'. Follow the single track in the direction of the white arrow crossing a stream which can be wide after heavy rain.

When the track splits, keep to the right and follow this until you meet a raised, rocky promontory with Loch Dubh a' Gharraidh Fail on your right. There can be a stream or water to bypass here after heavy rain. Continue straight on over the rocky promontory and you will see the Ringing Stone on the left near the shore. Don't be tempted to take a shortcut directly to the Stone as there is a sea inlet on the left of the rocky promontory.

Walk Details

Total Distance	3.7 miles / 6 km
Total Duration	2 hours

Terrain Description
Relatively flat ground with short, moderate slopes.
Can be very muddy after heavy rain.

moderate

Wildlife Watch

This walk passes through a variety of different habitats including *machair*, extensive moorland, known locally as *sliabh*, wet grassland, sandy bays and rocky coast, as well as passing many waterbodies of varying sizes – it offers the chance of seeing a wide range of wildlife.

Scan *Loch Riaghain* with binoculars for breeding wildfowl. Greylag geese are common here, but there are also smaller numbers of mallard, teal, red-breasted merganser and eider, whilst mute swans nest in some years and odd whooper swans may over summer here. Swallows feed over the loch edges from nests in the nearby farm buildings, whilst small numbers of lapwing and redshank feed in the wet grassland around the loch. Snipe and dunlin feed more unobtrusively in the wetlands but both can be heard singing here towards dawn and dusk.

The pools and lochans on this route are perhaps the best area on the island for seeing dragonflies and damselflies, which can be numerous on calm sunny days in July and August. Both black and highland darters will perch on rocks in the track to sunbathe, whilst four-spotted chasers patrol the boggy pools. Look out too for common blue and blue-tailed damselflies in the more sheltered ditches and in vegetation around the pools. This includes the beautiful flowering water lobelia, whilst the track itself has a range of orchids growing upon it including both colour forms of the early marsh-orchid.

A few eiders are often present on *Loch na Gile* amongst the greylags, which sometimes also harbours the odd summering barnacle goose. Look for a small island in the loch that is covered in willow scrub and bluebells, a hint of what the moorland might have looked like before the advent of livestock grazing. A hummock before the loch to the west of the track often holds a small mixed colony of herring and lesser black-backed gulls. Do not approach these as they will mob you mercilessly. After this loch, the route joins up with Tiree Walk B, so see that walk description for details of wildlife to look out for on the final coastal section to the Ringing Stone.

Calm, sunny, summer days are the best for looking for insects. Butterflies to watch out for on this route include the common blue, green-veined white and meadow brown, plus small tortoiseshell and red admiral around the farm buildings at the start of the walk.

Features of this Walk

This walk runs along the edge of Loch Riaghain and passes through an undisturbed area of moorland pools and lochans before joining up with the coastal path from Hillcrest to the Ringing Stone. The ground can often be wet and muddy after rain and the track along the western shore of Loch Riaghain can often be inundated. Stout walking boots or wellingtons are recommended.

Early marsh-orchid

Swallow

Formerly rare on the island, the swallow is now a common summer visitor, which breeds widely in Tiree's barns, sheds and ruins. The first birds arrive in April and large flocks build up in autumn prior to their migration back to Africa. Swallows hawk for insects all over the island but often concentrate over the lochs during cold spells. They are bluer above and have much longer tail forks than the sand martin.

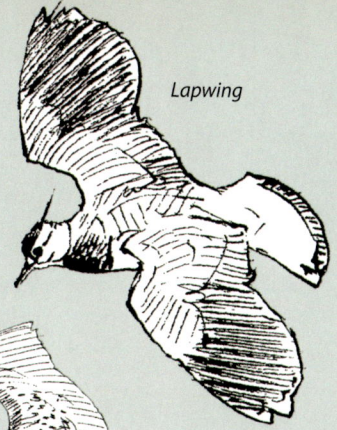

Lapwing

Snipe

Dunlin

Lesser black-backed gull

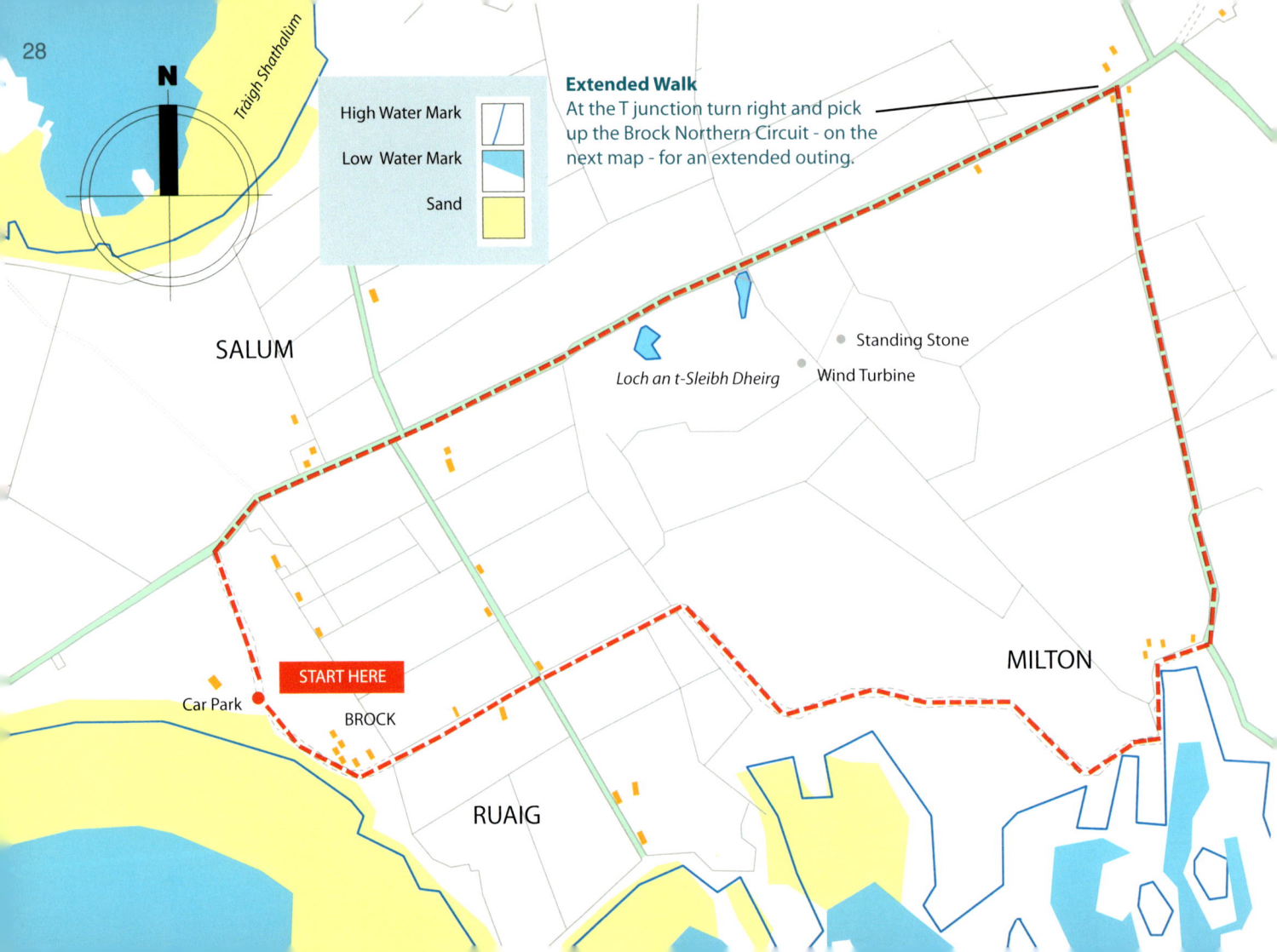

Tràigh Shathalum

N

High Water Mark

Low Water Mark

Sand

Extended Walk

At the T junction turn right and pick up the Brock Northern Circuit - on the next map - for an extended outing.

SALUM

Loch an t-Sleibh Dheirg

Standing Stone

Wind Turbine

MILTON

START HERE

Car Park

BROCK

RUAIG

Brock Southern Circuit via Milton
Cuairt a' Bhroic taobh Mhilton

E

A moderately long walk on good tracks and quiet roads although parts of the Ruaig to Milton section can sometimes be marshy and flooded after heavy rain.

This walk runs along the east end of Gott Bay, before cutting inland through in-bye fields at Ruaig and then rejoins the indented coast west of Milton. A shorter option after leaving Brock is to head north, up the Ruaig road, to the Salum crossroads and then turn left back to the car park.

Leave your car in the Brock car park.

From the car park follow a track past a group of several traditional felt-roofed black houses. Beyond the houses, veer left onto a farm track between two fences. Follow this, continuing straight on at a crossroads with a single track road.

The section beyond the road can be boggy. When you get to the gate, turn right and follow the now grassy track. After passing a large standing stone, the track bears left and then continues to meander along the top of a raised grass promontory. Just before the hill, at a yellow hydrant sign, keep right and then straight on. The grass track eventually reaches a gate at Milton harbour. Go through the gate and follow the gravel track to the road.

At the road turn left and continue to the T-junction. At this junction turn left and follow the single track road until the Brock car park is seen on your left.

Location

Milton

Walk Details

Total Distance	4 miles / 6.4 km
Total Duration	3 hours

Terrain Description
Relatively flat ground with short, moderate slopes.
Sections can be very muddy after heavy rain.

easy

Wildlife Watch

This walk passes through a variety of different habitats including *machair*, sandy bay, in-bye grassland, extensive moorland (known locally as *sliabh*), wet grassland, salt marsh and rocky coast, as well as passing several small waterbodies – it offers the chance of seeing a wide range of wildlife.

Scan the sheltered shallow waters and broad sands of Gott Bay with binoculars. Eider ducks and red-breasted mergansers are usually present on the sea, whilst both Arctic and little terns feed in the shallows. With luck you may spot red-throated divers with their fledged young in late summer. Autumn brings larger numbers of great northern divers plus passing groups of pale-bellied brent geese. Waders feed along the tideline and should include oystercatchers, curlew and groups of sanderling running like clockwork toys in amongst the waves. The more sheltered sands towards the islet Soa often also harbour small numbers of dunlin and ringed plover, whilst common and black-headed gulls are usually present along the shore.

The track up from the beach and across the Ruaig road takes you through in-bye fields where corncrakes can be heard in May and July together with the sky bound song of skylarks. Watch out for snipe flushing up from the ditches and wetter ground as you enter the unfenced *sliabh*, as well as meadow pipits, which will be the commonest small bird here. Wheatears and perhaps rock pipits should be present along the old storm beach and it is worth scanning the saltmarsh and inlets to the south for shelducks, redshanks and other waders. Mallards may be present on the small pools next to the track and the odd dragonfly or butterfly may be seen here on calm sunny days.

Milton harbour often holds a few turnstones throughout the year, whilst this is one of the few sites where common sandpipers breed on Tiree. Listen out for their distinctive alarm calls. A few eiders are normally present near the harbour whilst Arctic terns sometimes breed on the offshore islets here. Milton valley is a varied area of wet grassland and *sliabh*. Clumps of orange flowering montbretia dot the roadside and there is usually the odd pair of stonechats and reed buntings on the roadside fences here. The high road back to Brock offers fine views and it is worth keeping an eye out for buzzards soaring along the ridges and ducks and greylag geese on the roadside pools.

Features of this Walk

There is an excellent section of grazed saltmarsh west of Milton, before you reach the harbour itself. The route then follows the quiet road north up the Milton valley, passing through sliabh *and wet grassland on either side, and then west along the Caoles road. This road follows a low rocky ridge through the* sliabh *with great views in all directions. It passes a couple of small lochans before descending down to the in-bye fields at Ruaig and across the grazed machair to Brock. The route is generally dry except after heavy rain or in winter.*

Reed bunting

Red-breasted merganser

*These handsome diving ducks belong to the sawbill family,
so called because of their long, serrated bills, used for
catching fish. Only the males have a chestnut coloured
breast, the females have a greyish breast and brownish
head, although both show a short shaggy crest. They breed
in small numbers on Tiree's freshwater lochs but spend most
of their time feeding in bays around the coast. Females look
after the young and can have crèches of up to 15 ducklings.
They are gregarious, forming flocks of up to 30 birds
out-with the breeding season.*

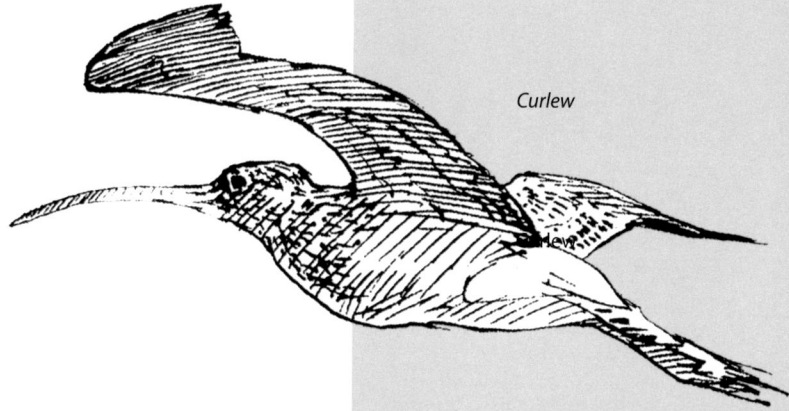

Curlew

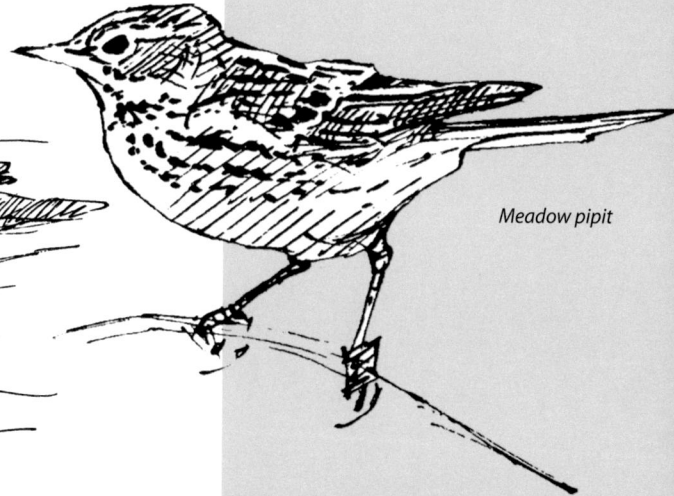

Meadow pipit

Alternative Low Tide Route

Dun Beag

Standing Stone

Wind Turbine

Stone Circle

Loch an t-Sleibh Dheirg

Eilean Ghrueusgain

Lòn Fhadamuill

Greasamull

Tràigh Shathaim

SALUM

START HERE

Car Park

N

High Water Mark

Low Water Mark

Sand

Extended Walk
At the T junction at Caolas, signposted Milton, link up with the Brock Southern Circuit - on the previous map - for an extended outing.

Brock Northern Circuit via Salum
Cuairt a' Bhroic taobh Shàluim

F

A moderately long, circuitous walk on relatively flat, dry tracks and quiet roads passing through Salum and Caolas. A variation along the coast can be walked at low tide.

Leave your car in the Brock car park.

Return to the road from the car park and follow the road east - towards Tilley the turbine. At the junction for Salum turn left.

At the end of the road pass the front of a house and go through a gate with a green arrow and a Tiree Pilgrimage Trail sign on the gatepost. Follow the grassy track, which meanders along the coast, until you reach two gates, one directly after the other, with a dry stone wall at the second. Follow the track beyond the gates, crossing a grassy bridge at another gate. Go down the track across a field to another gate. After this keep the fence and then a wall on your left to a gate at Miodar Farm. Walk past the front of the farm, respecting the owner's privacy, and then take the road to a rough crossroads. At the crossroads turn right and follow the road to a T-junction at Caolas.

Alternative Low Tide Route
Alternatively, at the crossroads, turn left and follow the track to a house and then turn right onto the shoreline. At the shore turn right and follow the coast passing several small rocky or sandy coves. Leave the beach and go through a gate up a rough track and over a cattle grid to reach the T-junction at Caolas.

At the T-junction turn right (straight ahead for the track end) and follow the single track road back to Brock and the car park.

Walk Details

Total Distance	4.7 miles / 7.6 km
Total Duration	3 hours

Terrain Description
Relatively flat, dry tracks and quiet roads with short, moderate slopes.

easy

Location

Salum beach

Wildlife Watch

This walk passes through a variety of different habitats including *machair*, in-bye grassland, sandy bays, wet grassland with pools, moorland (known locally as *sliabh*), salt marsh and an indented rocky coast with small islets, as well as passing several small waterbodies – it offers the chance of seeing a wide range of wildlife.

Skylarks should be heard, if not seen, on the *machair* north of the car park, whilst the short grasslands here also hold lapwings for much of the year. A few corncrakes breed in the in-bye fields at Salum, but easier to see will be hordes of starlings and a few hooded crows. The sheltered sandy bay usually holds a few eider ducks and red-breasted mergansers, whilst large numbers of common seals can be present at times on the small offshore islands. Waders feed along the tide-line and should include oystercatchers, curlew and perhaps sanderling, but better still are the muddy inlets to the east of Salum which provide rich feeding for mixed groups of dunlin, ringed plover, redshank and occasionally scarcer species such as grey plover and knot. The track east of Salum passes through an area of rich wet grassland with pools that are alive with breeding waders in early summer. Please stick rigidly to the path here to avoid disturbing the birds. Ideally view them from a safe distance or move through quickly if there are young birds on or near the track. Arctic terns and gulls also nest on the offshore islets here. Again please view these birds from the track and do no try to walk out to the islands at low tide, as this will only disturb them from their nests and you will run the risk of being cut off as the tide returns!

The track turns inland a little and passes the remains of an Iron Age fort or *dun*, which appears as a green mound south of the track in what would once have been an extensive lochan. There are more breeding waders on the marshy *machair* after Miodar Farm, whilst the road south to Caoles affords good views of Gunna Sound and the islands of Gunna and Coll. On calm summer days this is a fine spot to look for the fins of cruising basking sharks and the fins of harbour porpoises, and perhaps dolphins or an otter if you are lucky. Always present in summer are shags on the rocks and feeding gannets in the sound. The high road back to Brock offers fine views and keep an eye out for buzzards soaring along the ridges and ducks and greylag geese on the roadside pools.

Features of this Walk

This walk runs from the east end of Gott Bay, cutting inland across the Ruaig machair *and along a quiet road through in-bye fields to Salum Bay. East of Salum, the track passes several small pools and marshy areas that are busy with waders in spring/summer and affords close views of a complex sheltered coastline of saltmarsh, islets and muddy inlets, which are excellent for bird-watching. The route then follows the quiet road south from Miodar to Caoles, passing through more* machair *and in-bye grassland and then west along the Caoles road, where it joins up with the return section of the previous walk. The route is generally dry throughout the year.*

Lapwing

Dunlin

This small wader is present throughout the year on Tiree.
Small numbers breed on the central *sliabh, whilst larger*
groups, from further north, winter on the beaches and
flooded fields. Largest numbers however, occur on passage
in spring and autumn, when flocks of hundreds frequent the
bays and *machairs.* Look for the slightly down-curved bill
and the distinctive black belly patch in breeding plumage.
The buzzy "chrreet" call is very different from that of other
small waders.

Buzzard

Hooded crow

N

High Water Mark	
Low Water Mark	
Sand	

Please park in the car park and not on the dune tops. Access is to the car park only. Please do not drive around the *machair* indiscriminately.

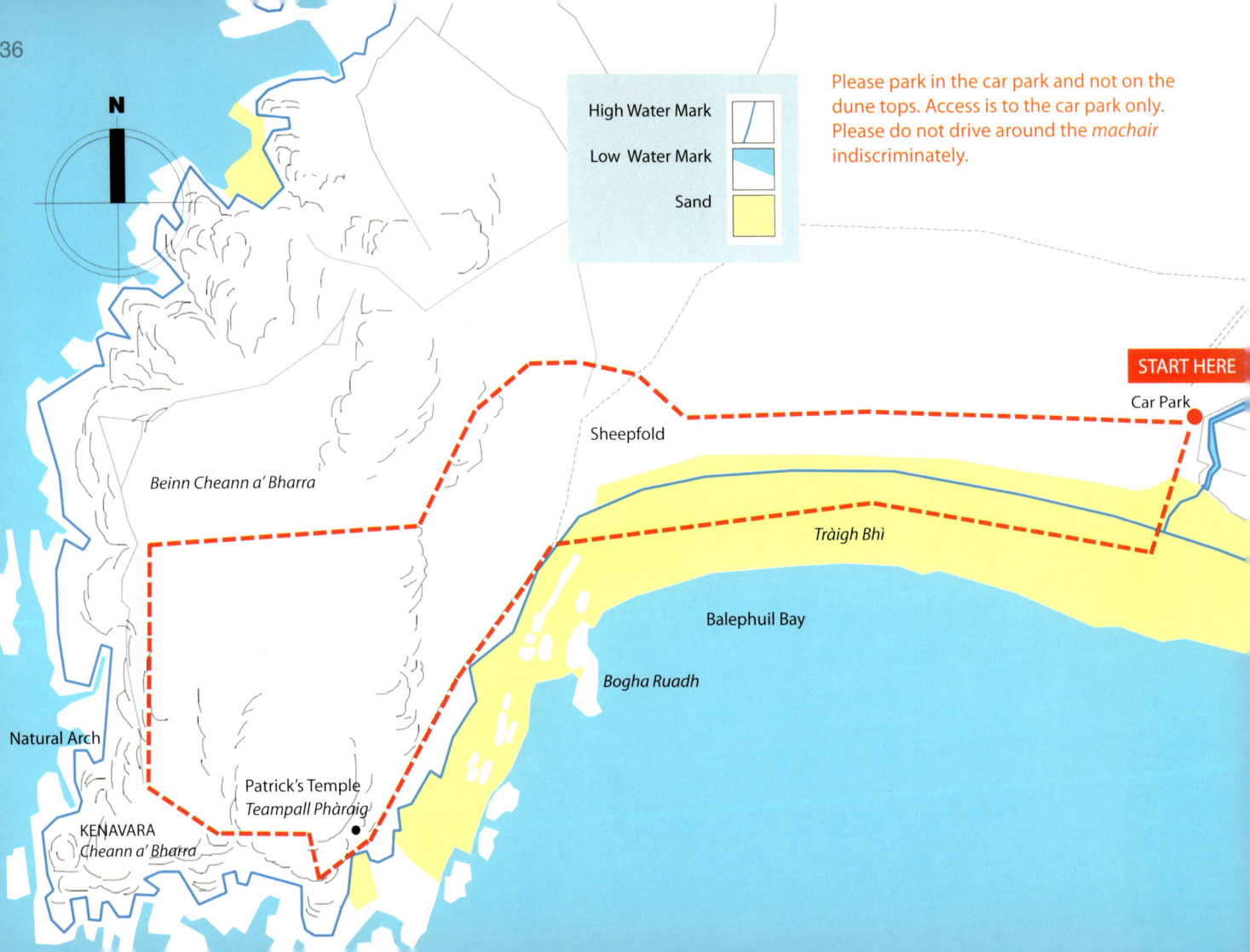

START HERE

Car Park

Sheepfold

Beinn Cheann a' Bharra

Tràigh Bhì

Balephuil Bay

Bogha Ruadh

Natural Arch

Patrick's Temple
Teampall Phàraig

KENAVARA
Cheann a' Bharra

Kenavara from Balephuil
Ceann a' Bharra bho Bhaile Phuill

A medium length, circuitous walk with a degree of uphill effort required, sometimes on uneven and marshy ground, from Balephuil dunes via Patrick's Temple and Kenavara.

G

Kenavara

Follow signs to car park behind the dunes at Balephuil Bay. Please park in the car park.

Take the sandy track from the car park onto the beach. Turn right and follow the beach until its end. On leaving the sandy beach pick up a track heading left through a narrow gully towards the rocky headland. A large flat grassy area is passed on the right - once the site of old kelp furnaces. Beyond this the track appears to split. Keep right and look for a diagonal cleft that can be used to pass through a rock band. Keep right beyond this and do not veer too close to the rocky seashore until Patrick's Temple is reached. An information board signifies the site.

Continue straight past the Temple and over a rocky step. Beyond this a thin grassy path gently climbs and then follows a grassy ridge uphill. As you approach the top of the ridge look left for a fence. Head to the fence then follow this uphill to the summit of Kenavara. It may be necessary to veer away from the fence and back again to make progress. From the summit continue straight on and follow a track down into a col. Keep to the right-hand track and aim across the col and back towards Balephuil. Alternatively you can continue straight up on to the second summit. As you cross the col you can continue straight downhill back to the beach. However, after prolonged rain, it is best to skirt left round the side of the second summit then descend gradually to the dunes above the beach. As an alternative to following the beach back to the car park why not follow tracks along the dune tops.

Walk Details

Total Distance	2.7 miles / 4.3 km
Total Duration	3 hours

Terrain Description
Steep sections to negotiate, sometimes on uneven and marshy ground.

strenuous

Wildlife Watch

From the parking area, walk to the top of the beach and scan the bay. Depending on conditions, a wide range of seabirds use the bay for feeding. Shags and eiders are usually present near the rocks at either end of the bay and fulmars, kittiwakes and auks feed further out, whilst on calm late summer days, small numbers of basking sharks cruise the bay. This can be a good spot for otters which use the burn to move between the bay and Loch a' Phuill; look out for their distinctive footprints on the sand. Ringed plovers often nest on the pebbly shore at the west end of the beach, so please stick to the path above the beach here during the breeding season to avoid disturbing them.

The short turf, rock ledges and wet flushes at the base of the headland are home to a rich variety of wild flowers including primrose and bluebell in the spring and bloody crane's-bill and northern marsh-orchid later in the summer. Wheatears favour the rocky slopes and rock pipits are present along the rocky shore. The steep cliffs on the west side of the headland are home to an impressive seabird city. Fulmars throng the upper ledges, with shags, guillemots and razorbills lower down and noisy kittiwakes in the gullies. There are one or two good viewpoints looking though the cliff top fence but crossing over this is dangerous and not recommended. Listen out for the twanging calls of twite which breed up here and watch out for great skuas which may dive-bomb you if you stray too close to their territory!

The eastern slopes of the headland can be good for insects on calmer sunny days. Common blue, green-veined white and meadow brown butterflies are all common here in season and the area can be good for red admiral and painted lady in migration years. The sand dunes on the return journey can seem quiet by comparison but watch out for sand martins and their burrows in the steep sand cliffs and listen out for the soaring song of skylarks on sunny summer days. The rare sea-holly also grows here and its pale blue flowers are worth searching for amongst the marram grass.

Features of this Walk

This walk passes through a wide variety of different habitats including a sandy bay, sand dunes, machair, rocky coastline, sea cliffs and rough hill ground. It offers the chance of seeing a wide range of wildlife including the largest seabird colony on the island.

Rock pipit

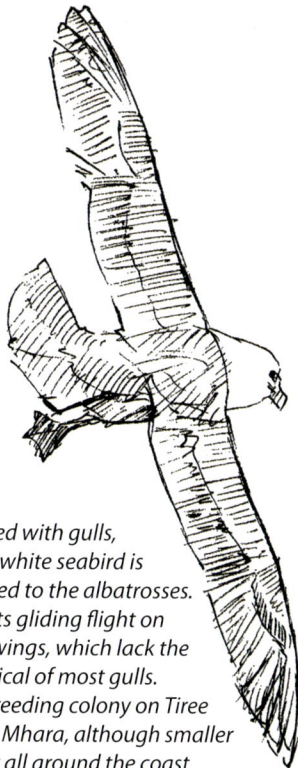

Fulmar

Easily confused with gulls, this grey and white seabird is actually related to the albatrosses. Look out for its gliding flight on stiff straight wings, which lack the black tips typical of most gulls. The largest breeding colony on Tiree is at Ceann a' Mhara, although smaller numbers nest all around the coast and on ruins inland. Fulmars defend their nests from intruders by spitting out a foul-smelling oil, so please give breeding birds a wide berth!

Guillemot

Razorbill

Guillemots

START HERE

Car Park

BALEVULLIN

High Water Mark

Low Water Mark

Sand

N

Hough Bay

Tràigh Hògh

Sean Rubha

Beinn Bhail' a' Mhuilinn

BEN HOUGH
Beinn Hògh

Loch Earblaig

Bealach na Beinne

Machair Hògh

Beinn Mhurstat

Dùn
Hanais

Walk Details

Total Distance	4.9 miles / 7.9 km
Total Duration	3.5-4 hours

Terrain Description
Steep sections to negotiate, sometimes on
uneven and marshy ground followed by
relatively flat, dry tracks and beaches.
Can be muddy after heavy rain.

strenuous

Ben Hough from Balevullin
Beinn Hògh bho Bhail' a' Mhuilinn

H

A long circular walk with some steep sections starting at Balevullin, taking in the summit of Ben Hough and the beautiful Maze Beach. It provides opportunities to see a wide variety of wildlife and flowers.

Follow signs to car park at Balevullin overlooking the beach. Please park in the car park.

Follow the single track road back through Balevullin to the T-junction. Turn right and follow the single track road uphill. After the cattle grid, turn sharp left and follow a vague, grassy path uphill, adjacent to the stone wall. As the path levels at a plateau look ahead and right for an obvious curving track. Follow this track uphill to a line of old concrete fence posts and walkway. Turn right at the walkway and aim for the derelict building - the old lower radio station. Follow the line of concrete fence posts and old steps up to the summit. Here you'll find the old upper radio station and look out. Please take care on the steps as they can be slippery.

Head south from the summit on a well-worn path towards the masts through a grassy col. Once the masts are reached follow the single track road to the bottom of the hill. Immediately after the cattle grid turn right and follow an old fence line. At the end of the fence turn right and walk to a small gate with a green sign 'Footpath to the Shore'. Go through the gate and turn left, following the worn path for about 50m to a farm track. Turn right and follow the farm track which passes an old concrete bunker on the left. A short distance beyond the bunker look for a vague path heading left towards an obvious sandy dune. Take this and head through the gap in the dune on to the beautiful Maze beach.

Turn right and follow the beach north. At the end of the beach go through a small gate on the left hand side of the raised headland, passing the remains of a *dun* on your left and then ruins on your right, and aim for a farm gate with a stile on the left side. Beyond the farm gate follow the grassy track which goes straight on and then meanders through marram tussocks. The track eventually widens. Turn left onto another grassy track just before the boggy area/iris beds. Follow this track for a short while until it meets a substantial cobbled track. Turn right and follow the cobbled track until it returns to the single track road. This is then followed back to the car park.

Location

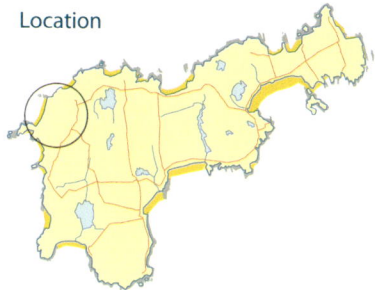

Ben Hough

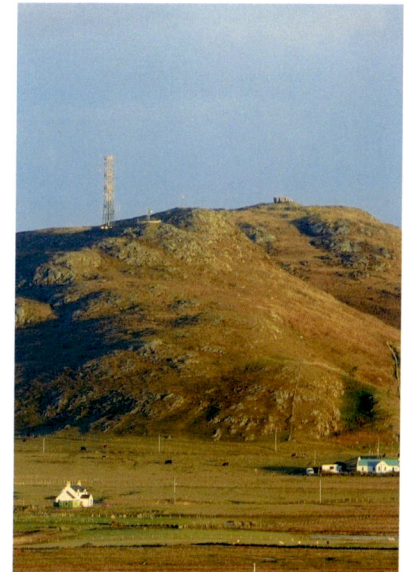

Wildlife Watch

The lower slopes of Ben Hough are home to several pairs of wheatears, which nest in the stone walls. Meadow pipits and skylarks frequent the grassy slopes, whilst rock doves often nest in the ruins near the top. The ridge offers splendid views in all directions. A few pairs of fulmar nest on the steeper cliffs, whilst buzzards and, more rarely, peregrines use the updraughts for soaring. A pair of ravens and a handful of twite are often present around the masts. Scan Loch Earblaig with binoculars below you to the west for breeding wildfowl. Mute swan, mallard and greylag geese are usually present, but teal and shoveler can also occur. The roadside turf, as you head down from the masts, is good for flowers including early purple orchid in early summer and field gentian later on, whilst these warm southern slopes hold many butterflies on sunny days including green-veined white, meadow brown and small tortoiseshell.

A few pairs of lapwing are usually present on the flat *machair* plain heading west from the hill and small numbers of gulls nest on the rocky lumps to the north of the path. This once thriving colony has dwindled in recent years to a few pairs each of herring gull, lesser black-backed gull and common gull. Oystercatcher, rock pipit and skylark are all likely to be seen on the coastal stretch of the walk but the real highlight is Hough Bay. This seaweed-rich bay can host a good range of shorebirds with sanderling, ringed plover and turnstone present for much of the year, plus grey seals and eider ducks bobbing in the surf. Winter brings purple sandpipers to the rocks and both great northern and red-throated divers offshore, along with a small flock of long-tailed ducks.

The sheltered dune hollows set back from the bay are rich in insects. The rare northern colletes mining bee has large colonies on south-facing slopes, great yellow bumblebees feed on the kidney vetch patches and common blue butterflies flit through the grasses. Watch out too for the pink spikes of pyramidal orchids in early summer, as this is one of the few sites for this distinctive species on Tiree. Frog orchids can also be found here with diligent searching. The flat machair plain that brings you back towards Balevullin can be alive with migrant waders in late spring, with whimbrel in particular favouring this area.

Features of this Walk

This longer walk passes through a variety of different habitats including rocky hillsides, machair, sandy bays and rugged coast and offers the chance of seeing a wide range of wildlife.

Common blue butterfly

Herring gull

Herring gulls are large, noisy gulls
that occur all year round on the coast,
as well as inland on the lochs and wet
grasslands. Adults have light grey
backs, white under parts, and black
wing tips with white 'mirrors' and are
much larger than the similar-looking
common gull. They also have pink
legs and heavy, yellow bills marked
with a red spot. Numbers of breeding
birds have declined by over 80% in the
last 30 years on Tiree, probably due to
changes in waste management and
fisheries practices.

Shoveler

Whimbrel

Teal

44

Haingis

N

Traigh Thodhrasdail
The Maze

Clachan Beaga

**Alternative High
Tide Route**

Creagan House

Kilkenneth Chapel
Cill Choinnich

KILKENNETH
Cill Choinnich

START HERE

Ghrìanal

Car Park

MacCallum's Cai
Tùr Mhic Chaluin

Please take care when walking along
the beaches from 1st April to 31st July
as there may be ground nesting birds
above the high tide mark.

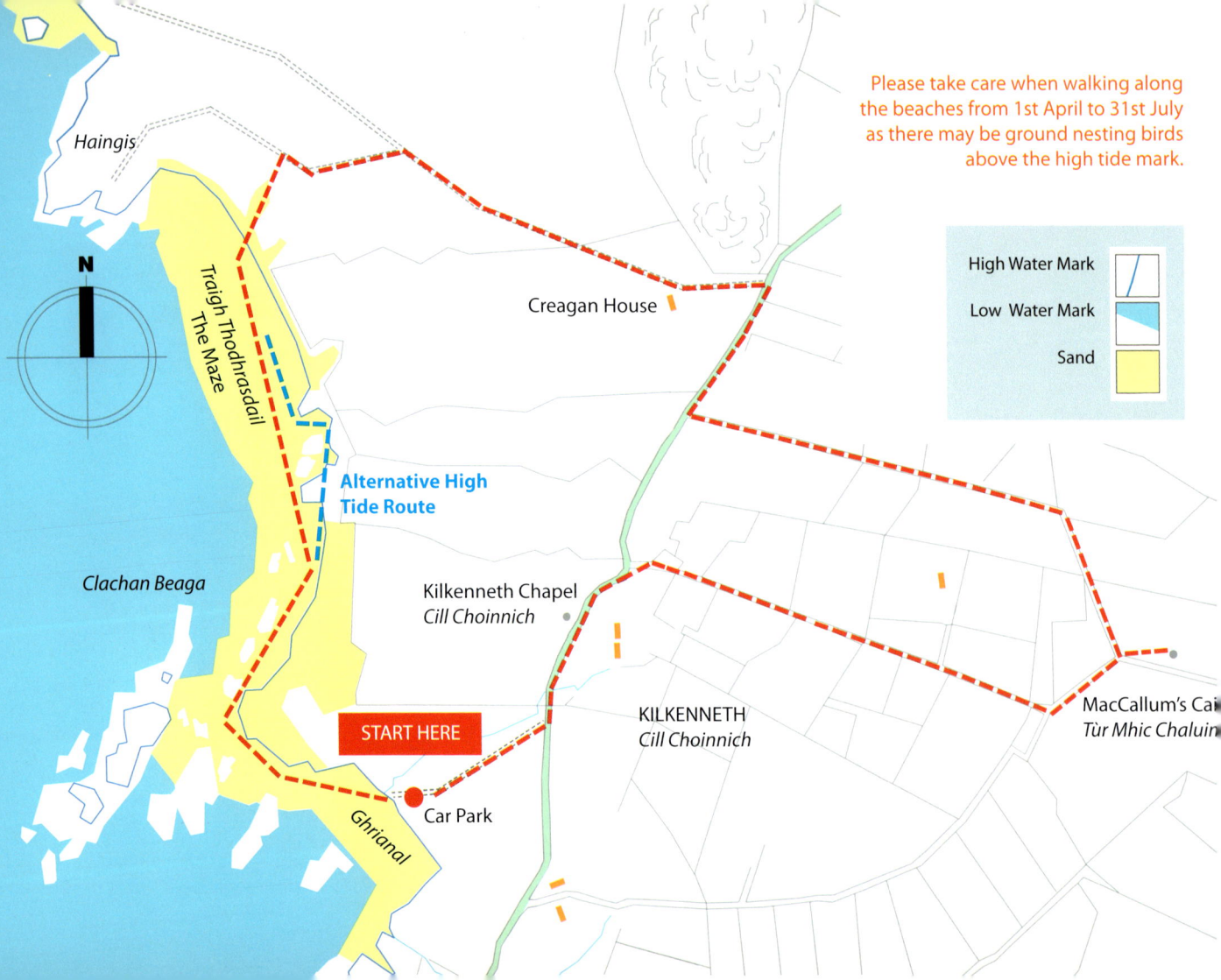

High Water Mark	
Low Water Mark	
Sand	

Greenhill, The Maze and Kilkenneth
Grianal, Tràigh Thorasdail agus Cill Choinnich

I

A moderately long, circular walk from Greenhill that takes in some spectacular scenery, which might require some scrambling over rocks to access the Maze Beach.

The walk starts at Greenhill car park.

Descend from the car park onto the stony beach, cross the stream and follow the track to the right which skirts the dunes. Walk along the open sandy beach beyond the point until a large rock band blocks the route. The rock band can be passed on the left at a very low tide but more often is negotiated to the right by ascending the dune and following a vague path to a stile. Go over the stile and then cross a small section of beach and scramble over another rock band. Beyond this you are on the beautiful Maze beach.

Towards the end of the beach turn right and ascend through a gap in the dunes. Beyond the dunes follow the farm track rightwards. When you reach the farm gate turn left and after approximately 50m go through a kissing gate. Follow the farm track towards the house and then the road beyond. At the road turn right, cross the cattle grid and after a short distance turn left onto a farm track. You'll see a green arrow and pilgrimage trail sign. Follow the farm track then a single track road to a gate on the left with signpost to 'The Cairn'. Enter field and walk to the cairn.

Return to the gate, cross the road and take the left-hand fork towards the sea. Follow the single track road which fades into a farm track. At the T-junction turn left onto the road and follow this, then turn right and cross the *machair* back to the car park. Alternatively, take a short detour to the west of the road through a gate, marked with a signage board, to view the ruins of Kilkenneth Chapel.

Location

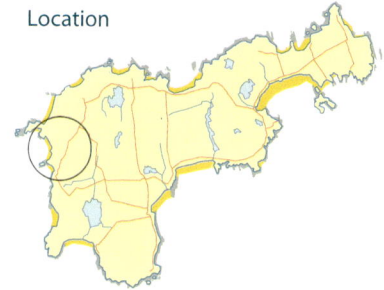

The Maze

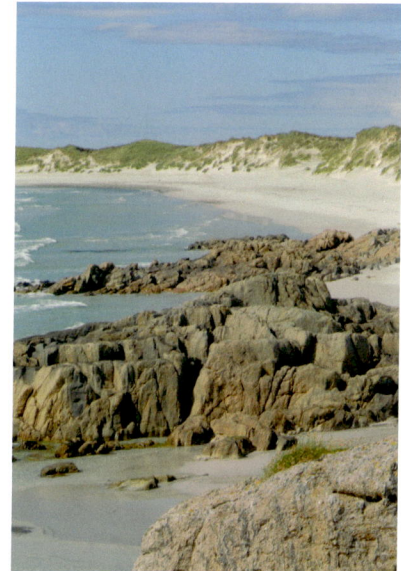

Walk Details

Total Distance	4 miles / 6.4 km
Total Duration	2 hours

Terrain Description
Relatively flat, dry tracks and quiet roads with short, moderate slopes. Can be muddy after heavy rain.

easy

Wildlife Watch

Scan the bay from the car park with binoculars. Eider ducks are usually present on the sea, whilst Arctic terns feed in the shallows. Fulmars breed on nearby headlands and often visit the bay, whilst common and black-headed gulls often wash in the stream where it runs across the beach. The sand cliffs by the stream normally hold a few nesting burrows of sand martins, whilst the odd pied wagtail is usually present. Waders feed along the tideline and should include oystercatchers, curlew, ringed plover and groups of sanderling in season. The coastal *machair* and dunes here are rich in wild flowers such as kidney vetch and wild thyme, which in turn attract bees and butterflies on calm sunny days. The huge leaves on the point belong to coltsfoot which flowers early in the spring. A few terns and ringed plovers try to nest each year on the point, so please give them a wide berth if they start alarm calling.

The lovely sandy beach of the Maze is often rather quiet for birds but look out for stranded jellyfish along the shore and for mussels, dog whelks and periwinkles on the rocks at low tide. The bumpy dunes that you walk through heading east from the beach offer sheltered sunny south-facing slopes, which are good for insects. Common blue butterflies and moss carder bees are both common and highland darters from the nearby stream often warm up here in the sun.

The track up towards MacCallum's Cairn passes through in-bye fields. Listen out for skylarks and corncrakes here and watch out for snipe flushing up from the ditches. Two elusive wetland birds, the moorhen and water rail, can be seen with luck in the wet areas here. More easily seen will be greylag geese, lapwing and mallard. Twite and linnets may be seen on the roadside fences and there are usually meadow pipits and sometimes stonechats on the moorland near the cairn. Wet grassland along the return track brings more chances for corncrakes and further wetland birds including redshank and reed bunting, as well as more snipe. The Greenhill machair often holds a large flock of golden plover in autumn and winter with the first birds returning in late July. These are worth scanning through with binoculars, as they regularly hold scarcer birds such as ruff and American golden plover.

Features of this Walk

This walk passes through a variety of different habitats including sandy bay, machair, in-bye grassland, grazed moorland (known locally as sliabh*) and wet grassland and offers the chance of seeing a wide range of wildlife.*

Meadow pipit

Stonechat

Ringed plover

Curlew

Reed bunting

Black-headed gull

This gull is a summer visitor to Tiree with usually only one or two birds remaining through the winter. Hundreds return in spring to nest in dense colonies in freshwater marshes and on loch-sides, where their harsh "kreaar" calls can be almost deafening! The dark brown hood of adult birds is distinctive, as is the white leading edge to the wing tip. Juveniles show a mix of ginger, grey, black and white, and are particularly striking in flight.

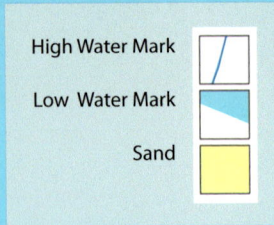

High Water Mark

Low Water Mark

Sand

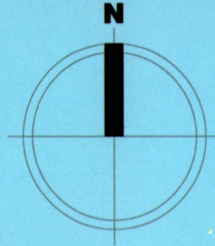

N

START HERE

● Car Park

BALEVULLIN

Machair Hògh

Beinn Bhail' a' Mhuilinn

Balevullin Coastal Circuit
Cuairt a' chladaich Bhail' a' Mhuilinn

A short walk on minor roads and dry tracks taking in the rugged coastline between Hough and Balevullin.

J

Follow signs to car park at Balevullin overlooking the beach. Please park in the car park.

Leave the car park following the gravelled track to the north west. As the track merges into the grass it becomes a faint sheep track heading through the rocky headland. Follow this keeping the fence to your left. As you approach a dry stone wall look for a gate in the wall and head through this. Beyond the gate head to a small rectangular ruin. At the ruin turn left and ascend a knoll to avoid a ravine. Pick up the faint track again beyond the knoll and continue across the machair. A barn, seen some distance away to the left, signifies the point to head toward the shore and onto the beach.

Follow the beach - sandy at first then with large pebbles. Beyond the pebbles a stile is seen up to the left. Cross the stile and take the left-hand grassy farm track. Follow the track, keeping left until it meets a fence near old war time bunkers. Continue following the track and fence line until you reach a cattle grid and the start of the single track road. Follow the single track road until a left turn, which takes you back to the car park.

This route has some boggy areas and requires scrambling over some rocky sections.

Location

Balevullin beach

Walk Details

Total Distance	4 miles / 6.4 km
Total Duration	2 hours

Terrain Description
Relatively flat, dry tracks with short, moderate slopes. Later sections follow rugged/rocky coastlines, pebbled beaches and quiet roads. After heavy rain some tracks can be muddy.

moderate

Wildlife Watch

Scan the sea from the parking area. Large numbers of seabirds may funnel west out of the Minch here, especially during onshore winds. Gannets, auks, kittiwakes and Manx shearwaters can stream past in their hundreds in the right conditions, whilst common and herring gulls are usually present on the beach. Calmer seas are better for cetacean watching, harbour porpoise and bottle-nosed dolphin being the most regular visitors.

The rocky shore west of the car park holds turnstones and oystercatchers for much of the year, with fulmars and ravens nesting on the low cliffs. This is a good spot for pipits, with larger darker rock pipits on the shore and smaller buffer meadow pipits on the grassland. The more sheltered rockpools and coast further west often hold a few redshanks and shelducks in summer – watch out for the tiny humbug-striped young of the latter, which have to run the gauntlet of predatory great black-backed gulls. Eiders and red-breasted mergansers are usually also present offshore here, along with feeding Arctic terns. The rockpools themselves are full of seashore life in summer. The deeper ones hold shore crabs, prawns and blennies, as well as sea anemones and a range of sea snails, whilst at low tide the rocks are covered in barnacles, limpets and various seaweeds.

The return route takes you back through short grazed *machair*, which can be alive with migrant dunlin and ringed plover in spring. Scan the small loch on your left. In wet summers the odd mallard or black-headed gull may nest here, although it often dries out in dry summers. Greylags are usually present in the croftland as you return to Balevullin, with wheatears on the lower slopes of Beinn Hough and swallows around the old barns. Pied wagtails, blackbirds, starlings and lapwings feed on the short grass at Balevullin.

Features of this Walk

This short walk passes through rocky shore, sandy beach and machair habitats, allowing a good range of wildlife to be seen.

Greylag goose

Red-breasted merganser

Manx shearwater

Starling

Oystercatcher

This distinctive black and white wader is common on Tiree and is often to be found along the shore. Large numbers breed around the coast and on inland grasslands. Many birds winter here, whilst others head south to Wales and England in the autumn, returning in April to breed. The long and strong orange bill allows the birds to prise open shellfish and to probe for worms in the sand.

Blackbird

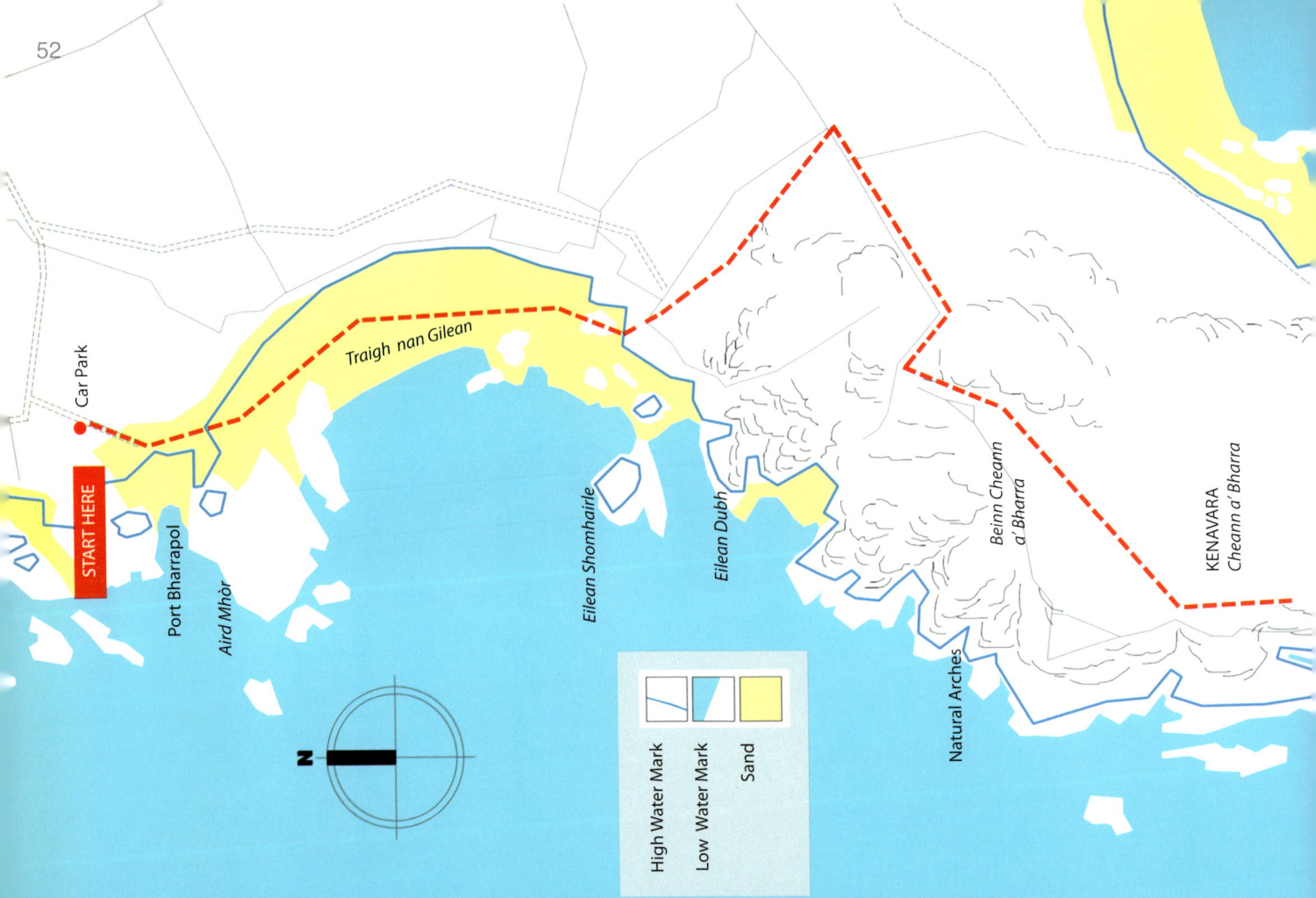

Car Park

START HERE

Port Bharrapol

Aird Mhòr

Traigh nan Gilean

Eilean Shomhairle

Eilean Dubh

Natural Arches

Beinn Cheann a' Bharra

KENAVARA
Cheann a' Bharra

N

High Water Mark

Low Water Mark

Sand

Kenavara from Sandaig
Ceann a' Bharra bho Shanndaig

K

This is a medium length walk with a degree of uphill effort required, sometimes on uneven and marshy ground, starting from Sandaig Car Park.

From the road follow the stony track and park near the information board and parking sign. Please stick to the stony track and do not park or drive beyond the parking sign.

Follow the track onto the beach and walk towards Kenavara. At the end of the beach a vague path leads left to a kissing gate with a sign 'Tempall Pharaig 1.6km'. Go through the gate and uphill in the direction of the arrow. Pass through the gate at the top of the rise overlooking Travee/Balephuil beach and then turn sharp right and follow the fence line and old wall uphill. When the fence turns sharp right continue following it to its highest point.

A small cairn a few metres to the left marks the summit of Ben Kenavara. To continue to the second slightly lower summit follow paths into the col and then up on to the second summit marked with a cairn. To return to the car park retrace your steps.

This route has some very boggy areas which remain waterlogged for prolonged periods after rain.

Location

Traigh nan Gilean

Walk Details

Total Distance	2.5 miles / 4 km
Total Duration	2 hours

Terrain Description
Steep sections to negotiate, sometimes on uneven and marshy ground.

strenuous

Wildlife Watch

Check the *machair* around the parking area for skylarks and meadow pipits. Curlews and oystercatchers often feed on the short turf, whilst wheatears and pied wagtails frequent the rockier shoreline. In winter this is a top spot for snow buntings, but in summer turnstones and ringed plovers are more likely to be seen along the shore. Walk south along the beach and scan the bay. Eiders and shags are usually present around the rocks and there may be a few Arctic terns feeding in the bay. Otters often use this beach, although their distinctive footprints in the sand are normally easier to see than the animals themselves. The sandy beach usually holds a few common and black-headed gulls, whilst this can be a good spot for glaucous gulls, especially after late winter storms. At the end of the beach scan the cliffs to the south. Large numbers of seabirds are present from March to August, although May to mid July is peak seabird season. Look out for shore plants such as sea campion and thrift as you head up off the beach and rock pipits on the rocks below the cliffs.

The steady climb inland should produce a few more meadow pipits with large numbers of noisy fulmars nesting on the steep slopes. A pair of buzzards often use the updrafts here. The rocky peak of Ben Kenavara is home to more wheatears but listen out too for the twanging calls of twite, which also breed here. The short turf and rock ledges around the peak host a rich variety of wild flowers including primrose, bluebell and spring squill in the spring, as well as mountain everlasting and heath spotted-orchids in the summer. Wetter flushes beyond the peak hold large numbers of bog asphodel, bog pimpernel and marsh lousewort in the summer, as well as a few northern marsh-orchids. The hill slopes can also be good for insects on calmer sunny days. Common blue, green-veined white and meadow brown butterflies are all common here in summer. The steep cliffs on the west side of the headland are home to a large mixed seabird colony. Hundreds of fulmars nest on the upper ledges, with shags, guillemots and razorbills lower down and kittiwakes on the steepest rock faces. Both gannets and Manx shearwaters may be seen passing offshore and on calm days this can be a good place to look for great northern divers in spring and basking sharks in summer. The cliffs themselves can be a riot of flowers in summer. Scan the cliffs with binoculars to spot swathes of red campion, bluebells and sea mayweed, plus a few localised clumps of roseroot. There are a few good viewpoints looking though the cliff top fence but crossing over this is dangerous and not recommended. Also keep an eye out for great skuas which will dive-bomb you if you stray too close to their territory!

Features of this Walk

This walk passes through a wide variety of different habitats including a sandy bay, sand dunes, machair, rocky coastline, sea cliffs and rough hill ground and offers the chance of seeing a wide range of wildlife including the largest seabird colony on the island.

Spring squill

Heath spotted-orchid

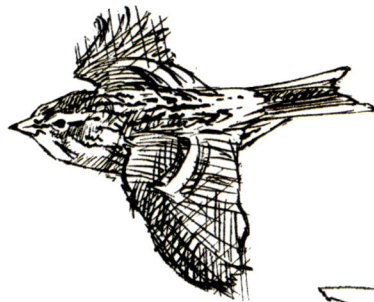

Twite

An increasingly rare bird nationally, twite still thrive on Tiree's well managed croftland and sliabh. Birds nest in small loose colonies on hill slopes and in rocky grassland where the males display together in a lek and show off their pinkish purple rumps. Twite are easily confused with linnets, which are also common summer breeders on Tiree but look out for their pale yellow bills and listen for their distinctive nasal "twanging" calls.

Kittiwake

Shag

56

SALUM

VAUL

Vaul Golf Course

START HERE

Car Park

High Water Mark

Low Water Mark

Sand

Vaul and Salum Circuit
Cuairt Bhalla agus Shàthaluim

A moderately long, circuitous walk sometimes with uneven and rocky sections.

Leave your car in the Brock car park.

Follow the beach towards Scarinish until a signpost is visible next to a small post box on a pole. Alternatively, walk along tracks behind the dunes until you reach the Gott *Machair* car park then use the single track road to the Vaul turning. Follow the single track road towards Vaul.

At the stone felt-roofed house overlooking Vaul Bay turn right onto the beach. A rock band toward the end of the beach is easily passed on the dune side. Beyond this cross the headland into Salum Bay - marked by wooden post. Continue along Salum beach. At low tide the rock outcrop part way along the beach can be bypassed on the beach. At high tide scramble up onto the rocky outcrop where a gate in the corner of the fence can be found. Continue along the beach towards the large white house. About 100m before the house an obvious wide sandy track leaves the beach. Take this to the single track road. Cross the cattle grid with a large grey barn on the left and follow the single track to the T-junction. Turn right and follow the road until the car park is seen off to the left.

L

Location

Skerries off Vaul

Walk Details

Total Distance	3.7 miles / 5.9 km
Total Duration	2 hours

Terrain Description
Relatively flat, dry tracks and quiet roads with short, moderate slopes.

easy

Wildlife Watch

Check Gott bay in front of you from the parking area. This is the largest sandy bay on the island and is internationally important for its wintering shorebirds. Large flocks of sanderling, dunlin and ringed plover feed along the shore for much of the year and these are often joined by bar-tailed godwit, curlew, lapwing and oystercatcher. Highest numbers occur on passage in May and August, when careful checking of the flocks may also reveal scarcer waders such as knot and curlew sandpiper. Arctic and little terns feed in the shallows, whilst the bay itself often holds great northern divers and eiders. As you head to Vaul, keep an eye and ear out for wheatears, pied wagtails and skylarks on the golf course to your right, which can also harbour feeding flocks of ringed plover, dunlin and turnstone at high tide and in rough weather.

Vaul Golf Course is also a good spot to see brown hares on the short turf, whilst corncrakes often call from the crofted in-bye land on your left. The gardens at Vaul provide some of the best cover on the island with nesting linnet, song thrush and blackbird, as well as wintering redwing, robin and dunnock. Greenfinch breeds in some years and this is a good spot for passage visitors such as goldcrest, willow warbler and spotted flycatcher. The piles of seaweed washed ashore in the western corner of Vaul Bay provide excellent feeding habitat for waders, with large groups of dunlin often present here and more sanderling along the sandy bay. Pied wagtails and rock pipits also frequent the seaweed banks with oystercatchers and turnstones near the rocks. Walk east along the beach and scan the bay. Eiders and shags are usually present around the rocks and there may be a few Arctic terns feeding or roosting on the offshore islands. Common seals haul up onto the skerries and with luck otters can sometimes be seen fishing in the bay. Crossing over the low point brings you to Salum Bay. Sheltered by skerries, the muddier shores here often hold grey plover, bar-tailed godwit and knot in winter with purple sandpipers and turnstones around the rocks. Watch out too for shelducks and eiders, which breed nearby and bring their broods here in June. There are usually a few Arctic terns and black-headed gulls feeding in the shallows with red-breasted mergansers further out. Walking east along the bay brings you to Walk F and the return to Brock via Ruaig, so see that route for details. The return route via Salum takes you past areas of grazed and arable *machair,* which are rich in skylarks, lapwing and twite in summer and host a large flock of golden plover from September to April.

Features of this Walk

This walks passes through a wide variety of different habitats including sandy bays, machair, sand dunes, rocky coastline and in-bye pasture – it offers the chance of seeing a wide range of wildlife.

Willow warbler

Corncrake

Knot
This squat, mid-sized, short-legged wader is scarce on Tiree. Small numbers winter on the more sheltered coasts, where they prefer muddier shores. Other birds grace the beaches and loch shores in spring and autumn as they stop off on their migrations. Look out for the brick red adults in spring and the peachy grey juveniles in autumn. In flight, the pale grey rump is distinctive.

Golden plover

Great northern diver

Turnstone

Tiree Ranger Service

The Tiree Ranger Service was established in 2013 to deliver a three year project 'Conserving Tiree's Natural Heritage' and followed on from Access work conducted under Tiree Rural Development Limited since 2006. All the elements of this project have now been successfully delivered. However, this has only established a beginning to the long term conservation of Tiree's natural assets. The main role of the Ranger is to safeguard and promote the island's environment.

By purchasing this book of walks you are supporting the work of the Tiree Ranger Service which operates throughout the year. Your purchase will help to finance a wide range of projects on Tiree:

- maintaining footpaths and disabled access
- giving advice and guidance to visitors
- youth activities with local and volunteer groups
- co-ordinating and booking croft sites
- coastal erosion control
- working with various organisations and individuals to help conserve and maintain our internationally designated *machair*.

John Busby • 1928-2015

The wonderful black and white vignettes throughout this book, which so help to bring the pages alive, were all drawn by the late John Busby. A highly skilled artist, John was among the very first artists to create depictions of wildlife that flowed with life and character, rather than appearing as subjects from still life. John was also an inspiration to other artists, who he regularly encouraged through his books on how to draw birds and through his annual Seabird drawing course in East Lothian. He was an immensely generous man, including donating a large collection of black and white wildlife vignettes for free use by RSPB. Personally, John painted a wonderful Seram Ground Thrush for an article that I wrote for BBC Wildlife Magazine. Without photos or ever having seen the bird, he somehow captured a perfect life-like image and typically, then sent me the original, which proudly hangs on our living-room wall. He will be greatly missed but few artists leave such an impressive legacy of work.

John Bowler

"My work is rooted in landscape and in the living birds and animals as they are part of it. I aim to show how creatures move and to express the visual delight they bring. I try to combine accuracy with artistry. I'm mainly interested in expressing the form and behaviour of birds and working from life"

Photograph | Dave Allan